FOOD MATTERS

GENETICALLY MODIFIED FOOD

by Rebecca Rissman

Content Consultant
Alan McHughen, PhD
Biotechnologist and Geneticist
Department of Botany and Plant Sciences
University of California, Riverside

Core Library

An Imprint of Abdo Publishing
abdopublishing.com

abdopublishing.com

Published by Abdo Publishing, a division of ABDO, PO Box 398166,
Minneapolis, Minnesota 55439. Copyright © 2016 by Abdo Consulting
Group, Inc. International copyrights reserved in all countries. No part of
this book may be reproduced in any form without written permission from
the publisher. Core Library™ is a trademark and logo of Abdo Publishing.

Printed in the United States of America, North Mankato, Minnesota
032015
092015

THIS BOOK CONTAINS
RECYCLED MATERIALS

Cover Photo: Parker Haeg/Demotix/Corbis
Interior Photos: Parker Haeg/Demotix/Corbis, 1; iStockphoto, 4, 11, 12,
18; Carline Jean/MCT/Newscom, 7; Vickie D. King/The Clarion-Ledger/
AP Images, 9; Shutterstock Images, 14, 25, 28, 45; SuperStock/Glow
Images, 16; Public Domain, 20; Tom Pantages/Newscom, 23; Glen Stubbe/
MCT/Newscom, 27; Saner G./iStockphoto, 31; Kicka Witte/Newscom, 33;
Richard B. Levine/Newscom, 36; Damian Dovarganes/AP Images, 39

Editor: Mirella Miller
Series Designer: Becky Daum

Library of Congress Control Number: 2015931577

Cataloging-in-Publication Data
Rissman, Rebecca.
 Genetically modified food / Rebecca Rissman.
  p. cm. -- (Food matters)
Includes bibliographical references and index.
ISBN 978-1-62403-864-8
1. Genetically modified foods--Juvenile literature.   I. Title.
664--dc23
                                                    2015931577

CONTENTS

CHAPTER ONE

WHAT ARE GMOS?

On an early June morning in 2013, a farmer in southern Oregon was stunned when he saw his beet field. It was ruined. A group of people had destroyed more than 1,000 sugar beet plants in the middle of the night. A few nights later, the group destroyed another beet farmer's crop. This time the offenders killed more than 5,000 plants.

Some people are against the growth and use of genetically modified foods and choose to protest them.

The community wondered why these events happened. The answer soon became clear. The farms grew genetically modified (GM) beets. The people who destroyed the crops were protesters. They did not agree with the use of GM foods.

Changes to Genes

Genes are the chemical building blocks of all living things. Scientists have discovered how to make small changes to the genes of different organisms. Doing this alters how the organisms grow, look, and behave. Plants and animals

Some grocery chains require suppliers to add a GMO label to their products.

with altered genetic material are called genetically modified organisms (GMOs).

Altering food crops is not a new concept. Farmers have selectively bred new crops for centuries. They choose seeds from the healthiest crops to plant for the next season. This results in crops with the best taste, size, and appearance. Farmers also create hybrid plants. One way they do this is by planting two different types of plants close together. Then birds or insects move pollen from one plant to the other. This cross-pollination often results in the creation of a new plant. Farmers hope the new plant has the best traits from both parent plants. But farmers are not the only people to genetically alter crops. Scientists use special techniques to make changes to seed genes. For example, they use the chemical colchicine to create seedless watermelons. And seedless grapefruit is made using X-rays.

Crossbreeding

In addition to crops, farmers have selectively bred animals throughout history. They allow two similar types of the same animal to mate. They hope the offspring has the best traits from both parents. This is called crossbreeding. Farmers might crossbreed a goat that has thick fur with a goat that produces large amounts of milk. Farmers hope the baby goat

Some scientists have crossbred bees to keep them healthier and more human-friendly.

will grow up to produce a great deal of milk and stay warm in the winter.

Creating hybrid plants and crossbred animals is effective, but the process is complex and can be very slow. It can take years, even decades, to get the desired outcome. For farmers who want new plants and animals with specific characteristics, genetic technology is the solution. Scientists can alter a plant's genes to make it healthier, tastier, and stronger. They can make it resistant to pests and chemical weed killers called herbicides. Scientists can change an animal's genes so it can live in different climates or grow quickly.

Despite all of their benefits, GM foods cause some people to worry. Are GM foods safe? Will they have any long-term consequences? Will they harm the environment? How will they change the business of farming? Government officials, farmers, and scientists are working together to answer these questions and more.

Crossbreeding All Around

You may be familiar with the idea of crossbreeding without realizing it. Many popular dog breeds are the product of selective crossbreeding. Labradoodles come from one Labrador parent and one poodle parent. Puggles are the offspring of pugs and beagles. Other breeds have slowly changed over time as well. This is because humans breed different types of dogs that have desired traits. Lap dogs, hunting dogs, and herding dogs are the result of selective breeding over hundreds of years.

As more research is done on GM foods, the benefits and issues will become clearer.

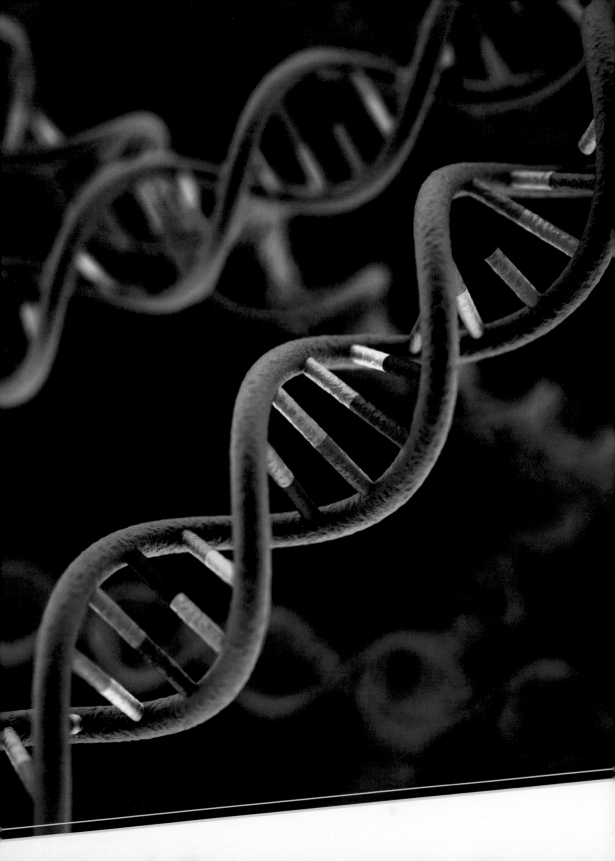

CHAPTER TWO

THE SCIENCE BEHIND GMOS

All living beings are made up of tiny parts called cells. Inside most cells is a nucleus. It contains most of the living being's genes. Genes are made up of sequences called deoxyribonucleic acid (DNA). DNA has four chemicals arranged in long sequences. The chemicals are called nucleotide bases. Each DNA molecule forms a structure called a double helix. This structure is

The order of the bases of DNA acts as an instruction manual for how a living being will grow and behave.

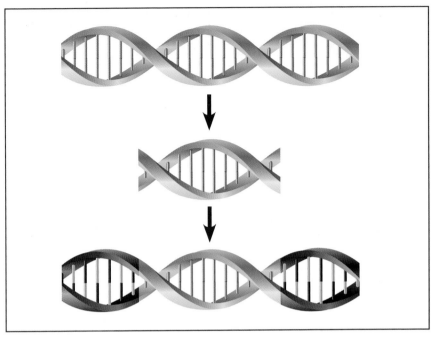

DNA Splicing

This infographic shows how geneticists splice the DNA of more than one living being. As you can see, they take a small portion from one double helix and insert it into the corresponding place in another. How does this graphic help you understand the discussion about GMOs in this chapter?

shaped like a spiral staircase. The chemical bases are found where the stairs would be.

Geneticists' Work

Geneticists study how living beings inherit traits from their parents. Geneticists can separate different genes. This helps them learn what each gene does. They can identify genes that control traits, such as eye color, height, or specific diseases. The ability to identify the genes has led to many medical advances. It also has changed the way humans grow food.

Geneticists can use their knowledge of DNA to change the genetic structure of different living things. For example, they may want to produce a corn plant that grows very quickly. Or they may want to create a strawberry that is especially sweet.

Geneticists make these changes in different ways. They can alter genes to "switch off" a genetic trait. This removes an undesired trait from appearing. Farmers might feel a pear's skin is too thick. Geneticists can

Mendel and the Discovery of Heredity

Gregor Mendel (1822–1884) is often called the father of genetics. He made important discoveries. Mendel bred different types of pea plants. He noticed the offspring of two different pea plants inherit specific traits from their parents. For example, when a yellow pea is bred with a green pea, the offspring is always yellow. Geneticists apply this theory to modern GM science.

Geneticists can change the way a living being grows or responds to its environment.

switch off the gene that controls the thick pear skin. The new pears will have thinner skin.

Geneticists also can insert a small part of DNA from one organism into the DNA of another organism. Tomatoes are harmed easily by cold weather. In the 1990s, geneticists spliced the DNA from an arctic fish with tomato DNA. They hoped this would create a tomato that could handle cold temperatures. The effort was unsuccessful. Since this experiment, geneticists have tried new combinations. They have combined bacteria and plant DNA to create crops that insects will not eat. They have combined DNA from microbes to create tiny organisms that help clean up oil spills in the ocean by eating crude oil. They have even combined human genes with bacteria to create the insulin diabetics use. This was the first GMO product in the 1970s.

GM Technology

GM technology makes farming easier in many ways. Some crops are genetically modified to be tougher and hardier. This means farmers will lose fewer crops

Some crops are modified to resist chemicals that farmers may use.

to disease or bad weather. Other crops are genetically modified to resist chemical pesticides or herbicides. This allows farmers to spray fields with a type of chemical without worrying about the health of their crops.

Plants are not the only living beings that are genetically modified. Geneticists are hard at work on new GM animals. One technology firm is creating a new type of salmon. It will grow approximately twice as fast as unaltered salmon. This new salmon could make fish farmers extra money. They could raise and sell twice the amount of salmon. This would also reduce the price of salmon and help salmon numbers in oceans.

Some GMOs are created to address world nutrition problems. Geneticists are making a type of rice that contains vitamin A. This will help people who do not have foods that contain this vitamin stay healthy. The added vitamin can help prevent health conditions, such as blindness. Other GM food crops are designed to grow in harsh environments, such as deserts. The crops will help feed large numbers of starving people in places such as Africa.

More advances are made each year using genetic technology. New medicines, heartier crops, and tastier foods are becoming available all the time. As geneticists learn new ways to combine and alter genes, their discoveries will change the way people live and eat.

CHAPTER THREE

THE HISTORY OF GM FOODS

n 1869 a Swiss chemist named Friedrich Miescher discovered DNA. However Miescher did not know how DNA functioned. Almost 100 years passed before this was understood. In 1953 an English physicist named Francis Crick worked with an American biologist named James Watson. They discovered DNA is shaped like a tiny spiral staircase. The discovery of this double helix structure was

The full importance of Friedrich Miescher's work was not discovered until years after his death.

important. It meant scientists could explore how DNA worked. As scientists learned more about DNA, they experimented with ways it could be modified. Geneticists soon began creating healthy living organisms with modified DNA.

In the late 1900s, genetic science grew by leaps and bounds. It developed so quickly that different corporations began to compete with their GM products. When a company has a patent for a product, such as a GMO, only that company can sell it.

YOUR LIFE
Is It a GMO?

Most people cannot tell the difference between a GM food and a non-GM food. Ask an adult to help you buy two papayas: one that is organic and one that is not. The organic papaya is not a GMO. The non-organic papaya is very likely a GMO. Slice and serve the papayas on two separate plates. Don't tell your friends which papaya is which. Have your friends or family members describe the organic papaya. Then do the same with the GM papaya. What differences did you find? Did you prefer the GM papaya or the organic papaya?

The Flavr Savr tomato did not last long on the market.

GM Food Safety

Soon genetic scientists became interested in producing GM foods. But first the US government needed to determine whether GM foods were safe. In 1994 the US Food and Drug Administration approved the first GMO for human consumption. It was called the Flavr Savr tomato. It was genetically modified to remain firm longer. The company selling Flavr Savr

GMOs and the World

Not everyone welcomed new GMOs in the 1990s and 2000s. Some people were concerned about how they might affect humans and the environment. The European Union (EU) made labeling GM products a requirement in 1997. Soon after, many countries in the EU made laws limiting the sale, growth, and testing of GM foods. More than 60 countries have strict restrictions or bans on the number, type, and use of GM products that can be grown and consumed. However as countries realize the economic value of GM crops and scientists support their safety, more EU countries are allowing them to be grown.

tomatoes could not keep up with demand.

In the mid-1990s, large seed companies introduced new GM soybean and corn plants. These crops could survive being sprayed with a particular herbicide. This was appealing to farmers. They did not have to worry about harming their crops when they sprayed for weeds. In the late 1990s, some GM crops were created to naturally resist pests. They contained toxins that killed pests but were safe for humans

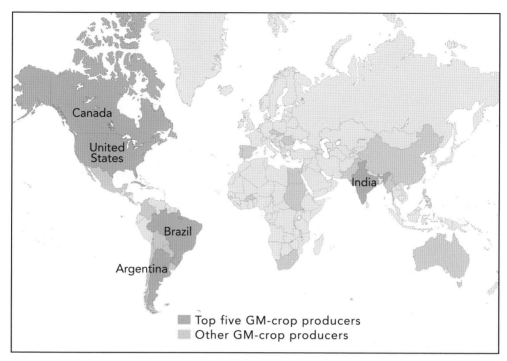

GMOs around the Globe

This map shows the countries where the most GMOs are planted around the world. Does the information in the map support what you read in this chapter? Does it show you anything new?

to consume. Both of these developments made

farmers' jobs easier. The pest-resistant crops also

gave environmentalists hope. Farmers growing these

crops could spray them with fewer chemicals. The

US Department of Agriculture (USDA) and other

government agencies that oversee food safety

approved the new crops because they would have no effect on human or animal health.

Resistance to Chemicals

One problem that occurs when farmers use chemicals to kill weeds is that some of the weeds develop a resistance to the chemicals. As more farmers started growing GM crops, "superweeds" became more common. These superweeds become immune to a particular herbicide.

After pest-resistant crops were introduced, some pests became immune to the crops' toxins. This meant farmers still had to spray their crops with pesticides to prevent them from being destroyed. GM companies are busily working to solve this problem. When farmers use GM crops as they are recommended, these problems are reduced. A recent scientific report found GM crops have helped farmers use significantly fewer chemicals over the past 20 years.

Giant ragweed is one of many superweeds that have developed over the years.

Geneticists are making new discoveries all the time. They are busy working to address the problems of resistant insects and weeds. But some consumers are growing concerned. Are GMOs safe? Or are they harming the environment and humans?

CHAPTER FOUR

PROS AND CONS OF EATING GMOS

M any people have questions about genetically modified food products. Because their genes are altered, some people wonder if they are healthy, harmful, or safe. Farmers, seed companies, scientists, and consumers may have different perspectives. To better understand the issue, it can be helpful to look at some of the pros and cons of GMOs.

Some people want the choice to eat GMO foods or not.

GMOs in Your Life

Some of the most common GM foods found in the United States are corn, soy, papaya, canola, and sugar beets. Because we use these crops for many ingredients, such as oil, cornstarch, sweeteners, and proteins, they are present in many foods. Read some of the food labels in your kitchen. See how many types of foods contain one of the ingredients listed above. Does the number of foods that contain these ingredients surprise you? A package may have a special organic symbol. Organic foods are not genetically modified. Try going to the grocery store and looking at how many foods contain an organic label. Does this number surprise you?

One pro of GMOs is they allow farmers to grow more food on less land. Pest-resistant and herbicide-resistant GM crops are especially helpful for this. They reduce the amount of time and money farmers spend on killing weeds and pests. Research shows that many GMO farmers use less pesticide than non-GMO farmers. Because GM crops often are designed to be hardy and tough, more of them can survive the growing season. This means

No side effects have been detected yet in animals that have been fed GM crops throughout their lives.

farmers lose less product and food production is more efficient.

Another pro for GMOs is they can be designed to solve specific problems. For example, scientists can increase the nutrients and vitamins in a specific crop. This means the people or animals that eat the crop will get these vitamins and nutrients. A recent report found that animals that have been fed GM grains throughout their entire lives and over several generations are healthy and have no problems.

Scientists are experimenting with other ways GMOs can be helpful too. For example, farmers can

Spreading GMOs

Sometimes non-GMO farmers discover their fields suddenly contain GM crops. And other times, GMO farmers find their fields have non-GM crops. When GM farms are close to non-GM farms, seeds and pollen can be blown from one farm to another. This can lead to the plants breeding. This means farmers are growing plants they did not intend to grow. Seeds and pollen blowing between farms has been an issue since the beginning of farming. Many crops have to be reasonably separated, such as popcorn and sweet corn or feed barley and malting barley.

grow flax and soybean varieties that produce more of the healthier omega-3 fats usually only found in fish. GM foods have been part of the food system for more than 20 years, and there is currently no information that links GMOs to health problems in humans. Most medical professionals in the United States support the safety of GM foods.

GMOs also have some critics. One of the biggest complaints is there is little evidence about how GMOs might affect humans. GMOs are still very new. Scientists have been unable to look at their

Many people against the use of GMOs are concerned their food is being filled with poisonous chemicals.

long-term effects. There are also questions about how GMOs are regulated.

Another argument against GMOs is that they may harm the environment. For example, one of the goals of GM crops is to use fewer chemicals. But some people believe GMO farmers use more synthetic pesticides and herbicides than other types of farmers.

Both sides of the GM argument raise important points. GMOs can be extremely helpful for farmers and provide presumably healthy and safe food for people to eat. However GMO technology must be used with care, and scientists must continue to learn more about it to determine if it has any effects on consumers. To decide if you support GMOs, take a look at how they affect your life.

EXPLORE ONLINE

Chapter Four focuses on arguments for and against GMO foods. The website below talks more about these arguments and provides more information about each side of the issue. As you know, every source is different. How is the information given on the website different from the information in this chapter? What information is the same? How do the two sources present information differently? What can you learn from this website?

Food: How Altered?
mycorelibrary.com/genetically-modified-food

Prince Charles of Wales delivered a speech at the 50th anniversary of the Soil Association in 1996. He discussed his hesitations regarding GMO technology:

> *At the moment, as is so often the case with technology, we seem to spend most of our time establishing what is technically possible, and then a little time trying to establish whether or not it is likely to be safe, without ever stopping to ask whether it is something we should be doing in the first place. I believe that this particular technology is so powerful and so far-reaching that we should seek ways of engaging a wide range of people and interests in a thorough ethical debate about how and where it should be applied.*

Source: Prince of Wales. "A Speech by HRH The Prince of Wales on the 50th Anniversary of The Soil Association." The Prince of Wales and the Duchess of Cornwall. Clarence House, September 19, 1996. Web. Accessed November 3, 2014.

Consider Your Audience

Read this passage carefully. Think about how you might reword it for a different audience, such as your parents or friends. Write two different versions of this passage, one for each audience. How did you change your tone and vocabulary for each group? Why did you make these changes?

CHAPTER FIVE

GMOS AND YOUR LIFE

Whether or not you know it, GMOs are a part of your life. More than 60 percent of processed foods sold in supermarkets contain GMOs. Processed foods are prepackaged and often contain many ingredients. GM corn, soybeans, and sugar beets are used as ingredients in many of these foods. GM corn and soybeans also are found in the feed cattle, chickens, and other animals eat.

Cookies, crackers, and breakfast cereals are common processed foods.

This means many foods contain ingredients from GM plants or were raised on GMOs.

Many people are not worried about eating GMOs. However some people try not to eat them. People who choose to avoid GMOs can buy foods labeled with the organic symbol. Meat, dairy, and eggs labeled as organic come from animals raised on a non-GMO diet. Another way people avoid eating GMOs is to grow their own food from non-GM seeds.

Political Debates

Many states are involved in debates over GMOs. Some politicians believe GMOs are safe to feed to people and animals.

Even though labeling is not required, many companies voluntarily label their products as "non-GMO."

Other politicians represent people who want to know how their food is produced. They want to pass laws requiring labels for all GMOs. Some politicians speak for people who believe GMOs are dangerous.

In 2014 Vermont became the first state to require GMOs to be labeled. Maine and Connecticut soon followed with similar laws. More than 20 other US states proposed labeling laws, but they were not passed. The US government believes GM foods are safe and do not need to be labeled. Many people believe requiring GM foods to be labeled will increase the price of these foods, which could impact people who have limited budgets. There is ongoing discussion about whether or not GM food labeling is required in the United States.

FURTHER EVIDENCE

Chapter Five has quite a bit of information about how common GMOs are in the foods we eat. It also talks about how some people choose to eat non-GM foods. What is the main point of this chapter? What key evidence supports this point? Go to the article at the website below. Find a quote from the website that supports the chapter's main point. Does the quote support an existing piece of evidence in the chapter? Or does it add a new one?

Top 10 Genetically Modified Foods

mycorelibrary.com/genetically-modified-food

Astrophysicist Neil DeGrasse Tyson was asked about GMOs at a book signing. He urged people not to worry about GMOs:

> *Practically every food you buy in a store for consumption by humans is genetically modified food. There are no wild, seedless watermelons. There's no wild cows. . . . You list all the fruit, and all the vegetables, and ask yourself, is there a wild counterpart to this? If there is, it's not as large, it's not as sweet, it's not as juicy, and it has way more seeds in it. We have systematically genetically modified all the foods, the vegetables and animals that we have eaten ever since we cultivated them. It's called artificial selection.*

> Source: Brian Stallard. "What Do We Really Know of GMOs? Tyson Wags His Finger at Critics." Nature World News. *Nature World News, July 31, 2014. Web. Accessed January 12, 2015.*

Point of View

After reading this excerpt, go back to Chapter Two and review the discussion about how genetic modification works. How are these two pieces of text similar? In what ways are they different? Write a short essay comparing the two points of view found in each piece of text.

- Altering food sources is not a new concept. Farmers have used selective breeding and crossbreeding to alter their food crops for centuries. New ways to alter food crops include genetic technology.
- GMOs grow fast and can be designed to solve different problems.
- GMO crops may allow for the use of fewer chemicals, but resistance to chemical treatment is a problem.
- Most medical and scientific organizations, as well as the US government, support the safety of GMO foods for animals and humans.
- People can buy organic foods, grow their own foods, and buy foods labeled as non-GMOs.
- Long-term data on the effects of GMOs on humans and animals is not available yet, since they are relatively new.

IN THE KITCHEN

Soybean Chili

2 large onions, chopped

1 red pepper, chopped

1 green pepper, chopped

1–2 tablespoons chili powder

1 teaspoon dried oregano

1 teaspoon garlic salt

1 can tan soybeans, drained

2 cans black soybeans, drained

1 can diced tomatoes with chilies

4 cups tomato juice

¾ cup dry textured vegetable or soy protein

Ask an adult to help you with this recipe. In a large Dutch oven, sauté the onions and peppers with the meat until browned. Add the chili powder, oregano, and garlic salt, then stir. Add the beans, tomatoes, tomato juice, and protein. Bring to a boil, reduce heat, and simmer for 40 minutes, stirring occasionally. Serve with your favorite chili toppings.

Tell the Tale

This book describes how repeated use of the same chemicals can lead to pesticide-resistant insects. Write 200 words telling the story of a farmer who is trying to kill these pests. Describe the sights and sounds on the farm. What actions does the farmer have to take? Be sure to set the scene, develop a sequence of events, and offer a conclusion.

Dig Deeper

After reading this book, what questions do you still have about the GMO debate? Do you want to know more about the tests scientists have done on GM foods? Do you want to know more about the concerns people have about GM foods? Write down one or two questions to guide your research. With an adult's help, find a few reliable sources about GM foods that can help answer your questions. Write a few sentences about how you did your research and what you learned from it.

Surprise Me

This book talks about some examples of GMOs. After reading this book, what two or three facts about GMOs did you find most surprising? Write a few sentences about each fact. Why did you find them surprising?

You Are There

This book discusses the many advancements being made in genetic technology. Imagine you are a geneticist who is developing a new plant. What would you make, and why? How would your new plant be different or better than plants that already exist?

GLOSSARY

artificial selection
the process by which humans breed animals and plants for certain traits

corporations
companies or groups of people who act as a single unit

deoxyribonucleic acid (DNA)
the hereditary material found in all living beings

herbicide
a chemical weed killer

hybrid
the offspring of two different types of plants or animals that have been bred together

offspring
a plant or animal's baby or babies

patent
ownership of an invention

pesticides
chemicals used to kill pests

sequences
the order in which things follow one another

splice
to join together or insert

LEARN MORE

Books

Franchino, Vicky. *Genetically Modified Food.* Ann
   Arbor, MI: Cherry Lake Publishing, 2008.

Genetically Modified Foods. Detroit: Greenhaven
   Press, 2009.

Hillstrom, Kevin. *Genetically Modified Foods.*
   Detroit: Lucent Books, 2012.

Websites

To learn more about Food Matters, visit
booklinks.abdopublishing.com. These links are
routinely monitored and updated to provide the most
current information available.

Visit **mycorelibrary.com** for free additional tools for
teachers and students.

INDEX

ABOUT THE AUTHOR

Rebecca Rissman is an award-winning children's author and editor. She has written more than 200 books about history, culture, science, and art. She lives in Portland, Oregon, with her husband and daughter.